The Old Ferry at the Black Rock.

BY CHARLES D. NORTON.

THE OLD FERRY AT THE BLACK ROCK:

A PAPER

READ BEFORE THE HISTORICAL SOCIETY CLUB, DECEMBER 14, 1863.

BY CHARLES D. NORTON.

THE ferry which once had its landing place at the foot of the highway now called Fort street, is the oldest institution in this city, and it is proper that its history should be written, in part performance of that duty which this Society owes to the public. From public documents and the laws of our State much of it has been collected, more of it from the testimony of early settlers on this part of the Niagara Frontier; and beyond the point to which their own recollection extends, they have furnished me with facts which were gathered from men who at a much earlier period found their way to the Niagara River. The old ferry was a crossing place at a period as early as the Revolutionary War, but whatever estimate may be placed upon the authority cited for this statement, the evidence of its existence in 1796 is clear and incontrovertible. By this crossing place many of the early settlers in Canada journeyed to their western homes, and over it the first emigrants into Michigan were carried on their pilgrimage to found a new State. The village of Black Rock is on historic ground, and so far as it can be said of us that we have a history, its most exciting events have transpired in that part of our city. At the risk of a digression from my subject, let me refer to a few of them in a brief manner, more as a hint to others for their collection and preservation, than for the purpose of detailed narrative. On the high hill or bluff that overlooked the ferry, old Fort Adams, or Battery Swift, was situated. There is now in the office of the Niagara Street Rail Road Company, a box of balls, bullets, and other implements of war, which were found under the soil in digging for the foundation of that building. The Maryland *Gazette* of December 22, 1763, contains an account of a battle between a detachment of English soldiers, who were moving from Fort Schlosser toward Detroit, and a body of Indians at the foot of Lake Erie, and the skeletons of Indians arranged in the form of a circle, with their feet inward and placed against a huge iron kettle, and their heads disposed outwardly and resting on hatchets, forming the circumference of a circle, which were found by Colonel Bird in preparing the ground for his present residence, evidently the burial ground of Indians killed in battle, afford presumptive evidence that this place was the scene of the engagement.

A skirmish between the American and British troops occurred at the junction of Sixth and Niagara streets, which resulted in the killing of Colonel Bishop, who commanded the British party, and the same foray came near losing for us the services of General Porter, who barely escaped capture as the enemy passed up the road to attack Fort Adams. They marched toward the residence of the General, which was upon the site occupied by the old Thayer tavern, now the residence of Rev. Mr. Robie, and would have taken him prisoner had not his housekeeper discovered the advance guard, aroused him from sleep, and enabled him to escape, half-clad, into the woods. Below this place, at the mouth of the Scoijoiquoides Creek, a part of Commodore Perry's fleet was fitted out under the superintendence of Henry Eckford, afterwards renowned at home and abroad as a naval constructor; and near by upon the bank the battle of Black Rock was fought about the same period of time. While I am thus indulging in a ramble away from my subject, the opportunity shall be improved of submitting to this Society the task of discovering the true orthography of the name of this creek, whether it is Scoi-joi-quoi-des, Sca-ja-quada, Scajaquadies, Conjocketty, Conjecitors, Unnekugua, or Unnekuguddies Creek, for I have found the name written in these various ways. It must not be forgotten that in Breckinridge street, near the old brick church, General Scott planted his cannon to cover the British armed vessels, which were in the stream prepared to attack the miniature but historical steamboat Caroline, on her passage up the river during the so-called Patriot War. It will be seen that the ground about the old ferry and in its immediate vicinity is not devoid of historical interest.

Captain James Sloan, a resident of Black Rock and a man of great intelligence and integrity, who has contributed largely to our local history in articles scattered through the columns of the city journals, visited the ferry in the year 1810. The field now occupied by the Niagara Street Rail Road buildings was then or had been an Indian field, for it was cleared and leveled, and on the south and east was bounded by a dense forest.

This venerable gentleman, who recollects with accuracy and relates with precision his early adventures in the west, full of stirring incident and exploit, speaks with enthusiasm of the view which opened to his sight when he stood for the first time upon this old Indian field. The majestic Niagara, with an unbroken expanse, bore its affluent flood to the cataract, between banks covered with primeval forest, indented with the scattered huts of the settlers on the Canada shore, and bearing on its tolerant bosom the wooded islands, which, in a bygone age, it had torn away from the protecting embrace of the main land. Under Fort Erie the British fleet, commanded by Commodore Barclay, was anchored, while a few batteaux, laden with salt, were moving sluggishly up the stream. These batteaux constituted the commercial marine of the river, whose principal business was the transportation of this commodity from Porter & Barton's dock at old Fort Schlosser, to the warehouse at Black Rock, or to the wharf under the lee of Bird Island, to be conveyed thence to Erie, then the principal commercial port on our lake. Few persons now living know anything of the history of the lake and river commerce from the year 1805 to the commencement of the last war with England. It consisted mainly in the transportation of salt between the places and over the route I have mentioned, to be conveyed to Pittsburgh.

Four or five vessels, each carrying from 125 to 150 barrels of salt, owned by Porter, Barton & Co., were engaged in business on the river, the proprietors of the vessels residing at Black Rock and Syracuse. When the wind was blowing down the lake, the vessels running from Black Rock to Erie were frequently wind-bound at the former place, and the salt would accumulate at Black Rock to the amount of 5,000 or 6,000 barrels, which were piled in tiers upon the shore of the river, under the bank, and remained stored in this way until they could be carried to Erie. The Black Rock was the great salt exchange, and the witnesses upon whose statements I narrate these facts say that it was not a rare occurrence for the Rock to be covered with traders from Pittsburgh. Captains of vessels and boatmen also met there to talk about business and interchange views. The Black Rock was a sort of commercial centre for the salt merchants, and in those early days the old ferry tavern was quite as distinguished on the frontier as the Fifth Avenue or St. Nicholas are in our time.

Two roads led to the ferry from the Main road to Batavia. The old Indian trail or path, which was the traveled way for the Indians going between the Genesee and Grand Rivers, diverged at what was then known as the Four Mile Creek, and pursuing the present route of Bouck street, came upon the river bank at the present Fort street, while the other road, called the Guide Board Road from the old cross-board, pointing out its direction, crossed Main street and followed York street to St. Joseph's College, and ran southwesterly into Niagara street. St. Joseph's College forms an acute angle with North street, and does not front upon it, and the cause of this is seen at once in the former route of the Guide Board Road, which ran directly in front of the building, and joined the present Niagara street at the residence of F. C. Hill, long known as the old Callender place. Niagara street had been surveyed, and the trees to some extent cleared off, but for the most part it was an impassable swamp, disagreeable to travel, though it was rendered comfortable in a very slight degree, at a later period, by a corduroy road, which old residents will recollect. The traveled road to Buffalo was by way of the ferry under the bluff to the lake shore, and over the broad, hard and level beach to the Terrace. Four or five years ago there lived at Windmill Point, in Canada, a very aged man by the name of Silas Carter. He had been a soldier in the American army during the Revolution, and while it was encamped at Morristown, he was in some capacity attached to the immediate family of Washington. He died at the age of an hundred years. Carter married at 75 years of age, and left behind him three children of the marriage, who are now living and have families. He was well known to Captain Sloan, who vouches for his intelligence and veracity. Carter told him that there was a crossing place at the old ferry during the Revolution, for he came into the country before that war closed, and that it was the only crossing place above the Falls. He spoke of it as a ferry, though no legally established ferry existed there until a later date. In 1796 it was well known as a ferry or crossing place. In 1800 Augustus Porter, then of Canandaigua, had a contract with the government for carrying the mail to Fort Niagara, and he says that his route was from Canandaigua to the Black Rock Ferry, and then by way of the Canada shore to Fort Niagara. General Timothy Hopkins, late of Williamsville, in this county, once said that he raised the first wheat on the Holland Purchase, in a field ten miles east of Clarence, and that he carried it in a wagon drawn by three yoke of oxen, over the ferry at Black Rock to Street's Mills at the Falls, and he complained of the charge for ferriage, which was twenty shillings each way.

Dr. Dwight, once President of Yale College, mentions the ferry in his "Journey through the State of New York," in 1804, and says that he "crossed it without inconvenience, though with much fatigue to the boatmen." A writer in the *Port Folio*, a literary periodical published in New York in 1810, in his account of a "Ride to Niagara," says that he came to Millar's Ferry along the bank of the lake, and notices the old route "by way of Bouck street as a short way to the ferry, if there be no object in going to Buffalo." The narrative proceeds: "The stone which bounds the river here is a mass of black chert. I arrived about 12 o'clock, M.; the ice was so thick in the River Niagara that it was impossible to cross until 3 o'clock, P. M. There were three wagons of emigrants waiting to cross the British side from Scoharie, in New York State, and Buffaloe, in Northumberland County, Pennsylvania; they were chiefly Germans. They expected about 200 acres of land to cost them $50. I understand the British Government sell it at $40 per 200 acres. The crossing here is three-quarters of a mile wide; half-a-dollar for man and horse. They catch abundance of fish with a seine; the family were dining on pickerel and salmon trout, each four pounds weight." The importance of the ferry, and the large business done there in the early part of this century is established by these statements.

The business at the ferry, and the peculiar advantages of the vicinage as a site for a village or town, alarmed Joseph Ellicott, for in 1802 he wrote to Paul Busti, General Agent of the Holland Land Company, saying that "the State at the last Legislature had passed an act providing for the purchase of the Indian possessory right to these lands," the southern part of which reached New Amsterdam, and adding "there is a situation on the lands equal to or better than that of N. A. for a town, so that if the State offers the land for sale this summer, before N. A. gets into operation, much of time will be lost to the future prosperity of the place." New Amsterdam was the name of the Buffalo Creek Settlement, and the southern extremity of the Indian lands of which he speaks was a point in the late south village of Black Rock, which, it will be remembered, once comprehended all that part of the old city situated between the State Reservation Line and the Niagara River; this line intersects the river at the foot of Genesee street. Reference will be made to documentary and other evidence in support of the antiquity of this crossing place, but let us now dispose of the Canada landing place. This landing place was always at the present site, and the earliest name I can find among the ferry men is that of Gilmore. He was a man of good family, who had fled from Pennsylvania into Canada to escape punishment for a political riot or fight in which he became involved. Captain Sloan knew him sixty years ago, when he lived on the Monongahela River, and says that he was a highly respectable man, and amassed property in Canada, owning a farm at Waterloo, but that his houses and barns were burned during the war, and Gilmore returned to Pennsylvania. Windnecker or decker was ferryman for a time there, and then Hardison, and perhaps some of you may know his widow, an aged woman who resides at Fort Erie. The ferry afterwards passed into the hands of Mr. Warren and Colonel Kirby, the latter of whom was a notorious character on this frontier during the war, and up to the time of his death, made it his business to protect his Britannic Majesty's rights, and see to it that they were not trenched upon by the Democrats over the river. Upon our side one Con. O'Niel was the ferryman at a very early day, living by the Black Rock in a hut which was at once his ferry house and home. In the year 1800 there was a tolerable road over the site of the present Fort street, leading to the river margin over a flat or plateau of land, about 200 feet in width. Upon the northern extremity of this plateau there was a black rock, in shape an irregular triangle, projecting into the river, having a breadth of about 100 feet at the north end, extending southward and along the river for the distance of 300 feet, and gradually inclining to the southeast until it was lost in the sand. The rock was four or five feet high, and square at its northern extremity, so that an eddy was formed there into which the ferry boat could be brought, and moored beyond the influence of the current. From this rock teams were driven into the boat over a connecting lip or bridge. The natural harbor thus formed was almost perfect, and could not have been made by the appliances of art a more complete dock or landing place. In fact no other part of our river or shore above the Falls afforded such facility for a crossing place. The river was narrow at this point, and the landing safe, and these facts create a presumption in favor of the statement that it was the ancient and common point for crossing the river.

This rock was well known, and had long been a fishing ground for the Indians. It is said that the herring came to the rock in such numbers that a barrel full of them was thrown on it with three casts of a large net. Near the rock and south of it, upon the river margin, was a plain or field, which was used by the Indians when they held their sports or practiced their games, while the wooded height above afforded to them a kitchen and dormitory. In a few years quite a hamlet grew up around the Black Rock, but it was not until the year 1810 or 1811 that any buildings were erected on the site of the present village. When Mr. Lester Brace visited the rock in 1807, there were no buildings in the vicinity except the Porter & Barton warehouse, at the foot of Breckinridge street, and a house which Nathaniel Sill had built on Auburn street; there was a log hut on the site of Albany street. The place wa· called the Black Rock Ferry from the rock, of which some description has been givens It was not alone a conspicuous mark on the river, but a well established business point, at which the crossing place or ferry had been for many years, and it gave its name to the ferry and the hamlet which afterwards sprung up at that place, not a trace of which now exists.

In 1802 the Legislature passed an act providing for the negotiation of a treaty with the Seneca Indians, the object of which was the extinguishment of the Indian title to the mile strip reservation on the Niagara River. This act recognizes the existence of the ferry, for it provided that the treaty to be negotiated should not prejudice the right of the people of the State of New York to the ferry across the Niagara River. To this act Mr. Ellicott refers in his letter to Mr. Busti, in which he expresses some apprehension that the future town would be located at Black Rock. This provision of the act implies, by fair construction, an existing and prescriptive right vested in the people of the State of New York to a ferry at Black Rock, and to have created that right, twenty years previous and continued existence would have been necessary, and if the right was thus recognized by the State, it will corroborate Silas Carter's statement that the ferry existed during the Revolutionary War.

By the treaty of 1802, made with the Indians under this act, the right of the Indians to use a crossing place at Black Rock is fully protected, and the tract of land bordering on the river, one mile wide, running from Lake Erie to Lake Ontario, is ceded to the State. The first statutory provision affecting the ferry, authorized the Commissioners of Land office to lease the ferry, with one hundred acres of land, on such terms as they might deem proper, for the period of eight years, reserving the right of the Indians in accordance with the treaty. This statute does not refer to the hundred acres now known as the Ferry lot, on the south side of which the present ferry is established, for this tract is north of the old ferry a quarter of a mile or more, and was conveyed in 1815 to General Peter B. Porter, to whom it was offered as a gift, but he refused to accept the title without making compensation to the State.

I have noticed for some time past that the stone monument which denotes the south line of the Ferry lot, upon the easterly line of Niagara street, is misplaced, and lies upon the street; it could not, without difficulty, be replaced; a survey, I suppose, would be necessary, but it should be replaced at once, to save future trouble in establishing the course of that line. In 1806 the ferry was leased or directed to be leased to Alexander Rea, but I cannot find that he ever availed himself of his privilege, for Major Frederick Miller appears to have taken possession of the ferry in that year, and retained it until 1812. During the interval the business of the ferry was steadily growing, for there was an emigration to Canada that increased up to the commencement of the war. The rivalry between the proprietors of the Holland Purchase, or, rather, between their agents and the proprietors of the Canada lands, was vigorously conducted, and the representations of the latter to the prejudice of the Holland Purchase succeeded in turning considerable emigration across the river. In 1812 Mr. Orange Brace became lessee of the ferry, but that was an exceedingly dull year; very little business was done on the frontier after war was declared.

It has been mentioned that Mr. Lester Brace visited the ferry in 1807. It will be unnecessary to say more of him than he was a son of Orange Brace, one of those hardy and resolute men who came to Western New York from New England in 1790, and to show that he was a man eminently fitted to be a pioneer of civilization in the West, it will be sufficient to say that in December, 1790, he returned to Connecticut on foot, with Judge Augustus Porter, and traveled a portion of the journey on snow shoes. Mr. Lester Brace left Bennington, in what is now Wyoming County, with an ox team and wagon, to visit the frontier on business, and crossing the Indian Reservation, his party were overtaken in the woods by a severe snow storm, which drove them under their wagon for shelter, and compelled them to remain there all night. Pursuing their journey, they reached Landon's Tavern, now the Mansion House, and turning into Commercial street, traveled by way of the creek and the lake beach, to Major Miller's Tavern at the old ferry. It was filled with sailors and river boatmen, who were holding high revel when Mr. Brace arrived, and the landlord, unable to keep them in order by gentle means, was administering such justice as each case required, and as the habits and manners of frontiermen amply justified. In the general melee

Mr. Brace's friends fled, seeking other quarters, and he sought the top of a whiskey barrel in one corner of the room, on which he remained until morning.

At this time there was at the ferry a house and tavern, with other buildings, making a promising settlement. There were no other houses at Black Rock, except a hut near the brook at Albany street, and the Porter, Barton & Co. warehouse, and the residence of Nathaniel Sill. Of this brook I shall be glad to preserve a memorial; it was a pretty stream coming from the forest, meandering between wooded banks, and at Niagara street it rushed over a broken ledge of rocks in mimic falls, and poured its crystal water into the ungrateful Niagara. A few years ago this laughing stream was turned into a sewer, and now mingles its turbid and muddy waters with the Erie Canal.

Major Miller's lease for an unexpired term of two years was transferred to Orange Dean and Holden Allen, the latter of whom raised a family of stalwart boys, who became sailors and lake captains, and Captain Levi Allen of this city, with two of his brothers, are survivors of this family. Doubtless there are many facts which have escaped my observation that would have rendered this history more interesting. The men who lived upon the frontier at that time possessed many admirable qualities; they were bold, accustomed to danger, self-reliant, fertile in resources, and full of that rude energy which clears up forests, lays the foundation of towns, and makes way for that more refined civilization which, if it has more of the grace of life, has less real energy and practical sense. It is certainly desirable that sketches of these men should be preserved, for the early history of Western New York is found in the narrative of the enterprise, the thrift and industry, and the personal sacrifices of the early pioneers. In 1812 the State resumed charge of the old ferry, and by an act of that year directed the leasing of it by the commissioners of the land office, reserving the Indian rights as provided by the treaty. I dismiss the Indians with the remark that this right of free ferriage was reserved to them in all the leases, and I have found no law which deprives them of their ancient privilege.

The war cloud began to lower over the border, and the frontier men heard the sound of approaching conflict. The business at the old ferry had been steadily increasing, but entirely ceased at the commencement of actual hostilities. The emigration into Canada had been considerable; the large four horse wagons, with their singular loads, were constant visitors at the ferry; there had been frequent crossing to deal at Dongas's store, at Fort Erie, at which place the settlers bought their glass and nails, and on the whole the ferrymen at the Black Rock had been greatly benefited, and were rejoicing in growing profits.

A store or grocery had been established; there were other shops at the Rock, and among others who had found their way to the place was Mr. E. D. Efner, to whom you will need no introduction. General Sylvester Mathews, who was a well known man here twenty-five years ago, and Loren Hodge and his father, resided once at the old ferry. Fifty years have passed, and the mutability of earthly things receives a forcible illustration in the changes at this place. The canal has obliterated the famous black rock, the rail road runs over the site of the old ferry house and tavern, and the pier cuts in twain the river which once unfolded its regal amplitude between the opposing shores; Squaw Island, once heavily wooded and filled with game, denuded of its forest glories, spreads upon the river a patch of unsightly meadow and swamp land; Bird Island has quite gone out of sight; old Fort Erie is a mouldering ruin; and the only improvement upon the scene is the flourishing commercial city to whose local history this contribution is made.

This paper shall be closed before the time is entirely exhausted, by recounting the further history of the old ferry from the memoranda of Mr. Lester Brace. In 1813, to use an expression then prevalent, "the lines were opened," which means that it had become safe for Americans to venture upon business along the river, and Mr. Brace and Mr. St. John, who is represented in this city by numerous descendants, thought that something could be done with the ferry. They bought Hardison's boats, and resumed the business of carriers between Canada and the Black Rock. The business was inaugurated by a sad catastrophe which awakened the sympathy of the whole settlement at Buffalo and the Black Rock. On the 6th of June, 1813, a clear cold morning, with the ice running in the river, Mr. Brace, with Mr. St. John, to whom the management of the boat was entrusted as the more skillful navigator, started from the rock to cross the river. The boat was a scow of about ten tons burthen, propelled by sweeps handled by two or four men, and steered by another long sweep at the stern. The route was directly across the stream, and then the ferryman dropped down to the wharf, at the present ferry landing. At times this was difficult to accomplish, particularly when ice was running in the river, and the boat was often carried down to a point near or opposite Squaw Island, which obliged the boatmen to cross and pole up the river to the Black Rock, a laborious and very wearisome task. Two or three of Commodore Perry's vessels, which had been fitted out by Henry Eckford at the mouth of the Scoijoiquoidies Creek, had made an attempt to get up the Niagara into the lake, to join the squadron, but were obliged to cast anchor in the very path of the ferry boat. The ferryman had been advised that it was venturesome to attempt to go above the vessels in order to reach the Canada landing, but Mr. St. John, relying on his skill as a boatman and his knowledge of the river, supposed that he could accomplish it without collision. He had not overrated his knowledge or his skill, but an unforeseen danger presented itself, which was discovered too late to be avoided. The ferry boat would have cleared the foremost vessel, but it was driven upon the cable which held her at anchor, and the play of the cable as it undulated with the motion of the vessel, upset the ferry boat and turned the whole party into the river. The boats of the ship nearest them had gone to Buffalo Creek, and the party, which consisted of Mr. Brace and Mr. St. John and his son, four soldiers, and four other passengers, one of them having a horse with him, were in imminent danger of drowning. Mr. St. John went down, but rose again, and spoke encouraging words to Mr. Brace, putting his hands on his shoulder at the same time, but suddenly sunk and was drowned; his son, a fine athletic young man, had nearly reached shallow water when he disappeared, and Mr. Brace grasped a board, by means of which his life was saved. There was another incident which is worthy of preservation. One day there came to the ferry a number of villagers from Buffalo, who desired to cross to Canada. Dr. Josiah Trowbridge and Mr. Bemis were of the company. It was a cold December day, and Mr. Brace was averse to crossing, for he was unwell, and there had been rumors which, if true, rendered a visit to the other side somewhat hazardous. Dr. Trowbridge was quite urgent, however, for his business on the Canada shore was impelled by the same motive which induced Leander to swim the Hellespont. Mr. Brace saw the white flag flying on the Canada side, and after some hesitation, consented to allow his brother-in-law, Arden Merrill, to take his place in the boat and ferry the travelers to the other shore. As the ferry boat approached the Canada landing, two or three sleighs filled with men were approaching from below, but the matter excited neither suspicion nor alarm. The passengers had hardly landed when they were seized as prisoners, with the exception of Dr. Trowbridge and Mr. Pomeroy, who escaped to the woods. The British party then fired into the boat, which had moved from the shore into the river. Merrill, the brother-in-law of Mr. Brace, was killed; his body, stripped of boots and watch, was afterwards recovered by a flag of truce. One of the passengers was never afterwards heard of; another was carried away as a prisoner, and subsequently released at Halifax.

Dr. Trowbridge and his companions found their way to Baxter's, six miles above the ferry, and there seized upon a boat against the remonstrance of the proprietor, who was not disposed to aid their escape, and got safely back to Buffalo Creek. This was a most unprovoked and unjustifiable outrage, not the only one perpetrated by the enemy during that war. The people on the ferry boat had trusted to the white flag flying at the ferry landing, and had they crossed the river without that protection, there was no excuse for the firing, as they were unarmed and might have been taken prisoners without loss of life.

The ferry was then discontinued and the boats sunk at the mouth of the Scoijoiquoides Creek, from which they were taken by the British in one of their marauding excursions, and carried over to Canada. They were retaken by our army and used for government purposes, and Mr. Brace found them in possession of Major Barton, the United States Quartermaster, who refused to deliver them to him, alleging that the boats had been captured from the enemy and were the property of the government. Mr. Brace, not caring to dispute the quartermaster's law, paid $100 to get them again, and in 1815, on the declaration of peace, opened his tavern and resumed his ferry, and continued there until 1821. That he had been prospered in his business appears from the nett income of his tavern and ferry, which, in 1813, was $3,000. For a number of years it continued to yield a handsome revenue, larger, upon an average, than has since been derived from the present ferry.

Among the persons who boarded with Mr. Brace at the old ferry, was Captain James Rough, a Scotchman by birth and a mariner by profession. He was one of the earliest navigators of the western lakes, and had been in the employ of John Jacob Astor when he had a fur trading house at Mackinac. He died at Black Rock at an advanced age, and is buried in the old Guide Board Road Cemetery. His friend, Major Donald Fraser, placed at the head of his grave a small willow, which has grown to be a large tree, and the inscription on his tombstone closes with the following lines:

Here, moored beneath this willow tree,
Lies honor, worth, and integrity.
More I might add, but 'tis enough;
They concentered all in honest Rough.
With such as he,
Where'er he be,
May I be saved
Or d—d.

In 1821 the ferry was transferred to Asa Stannard, the father of a race of sons, some of whom became identified with our lake marine, and were well known to the dock merchants of an early day. The present Member of Assembly from the First District is a son of Asa Stannard.

In 1822 or 1824 the old ferry ceased to exist; the act of authorizing the lease to Stannard provides that "if the ferry is injured by the construction of the Great Western Canal," Stannard should be compensated for improvements but not for loss of profits. The same act gave Stannard an extension of the lease if he would build a horse boat for purposes of ferriage. Mr. Stannard did not build the boat to be propelled by horse power, which the act of the Legislature contemplated, but continued to use the scow rowed by four men with two oars, and to cross at the old place until the construction of the canal rendered it necessary to remove the ferry to another point.

In 1824 the old ferry, for so long a time a place of such importance, and which had already assumed the appearance of a village, was deserted. The great rock, a land mark known to all the settlers on this part of the Holland Purchase, and to all travelers on the river, was blown up, the old road was neglected and became impassable, the houses gradually fell into ruin, and to-day there is nothing on the spot to indicate its former existence.

The ferry was removed to a point of land at the foot of what is now Ferry street, on the south line of the ferry lot, and in 1826 Donald Fraser and Lester Brace became the lessees, but the rapid march of invention and improvement rendered it necessary that the old scow ferry boat should give way to more rapid method of propulsion, and Brace and Fraser were bound to put upon the river, within one year, a steam or horse boat.

If it were within the scope of my subject, it would be a pleasant duty to give some reminiscence of Donald Fraser; he had witnessed different vicissitudes of fortune, and had survived them all without losing that exuberant good nature which was a remarkable quality in his character. From early youth he was a courageous and gallant soldier; he had been aid to General Pike at the siege and conquest of Little York, (now Toronto,) and was with him when he fell on that memorable occasion. In the same capacity he had served under General Winder when the latter was taken prisoner during the last war with Great Britain; and at the sortie of Fort Erie as aid to General Porter, his gallantry and soldierly conduct received the most flattering notice in the despatches of the General to the Commander-in-Chief. Major Fraser was afterwards on the staff of General Brown, after which he served at Fort Niagara, and at a later period acted as Secretary to General Porter while he was engaged as Commissioner in surveying and establishing the northern boundary between the United States and Canada, under the treaty of Ghent. He was a Scotchman, the member of a celebrated clan, and full of genial and generous feeling toward all mankind. His ferry house and store was a museum of curiosities. At the door the public were informed that "Folks were married here," and the house was filled with articles, the most of which were unsaleable, presenting a ludicrous yet remarkable collection of odd things; in the strictest sense of the word it was a curiosity shop. The residents of thirty years ago will recollect his sleigh rides, in a bark canoe mounted on runners, with a stuffed deer standing at the prow, and ten or twelve men habited in Indian costume paddling furiously as they dashed through the streets at the full speed of four horses, ridden by four impromptu savages. After the death of Captain Rough, Major Fraser disguised himself, and calling upon the prominent citizens of the village, represented himself to be the sole heir of the deceased, just arrived from Scotland. He was so successfully disguised in every respect, and his claims were apparently so well founded and sustained, that no question was made about his taking possession of the estate, which was considerable, and his friends and acquaintances recognized him as the heir of Captain Rough, and the owner of his late estate. A paper might be filled with reminiscences of this singular man, but space can only be allowed to say that after his removal from Black Rock he was in the army as quartermaster, and died a few years ago an officer at the New York Custom House. Messrs. Brace and Fraser placed a horse boat on the river, Mr. Brace making the journey to Albany to ascertain the merits of the novel invention which the Legislature required the ferry lessees to adopt, and he brought back the machinery for his boat. It was nothing more than a wheel upon a horizontal plane, resting on the main shaft, which it propelled by means of cogs playing into cogs upon the shaft; four horses treading the wheel being the propelling power. It was a great invention for that time, and was the second boat of the kind ever used in this country.

In 1840 James Haggart became the lessee of the ferry and the successor of Brace and Fraser, and placed a steam ferry boat on the river, in accordance with the provisions of an act of the Legislature granting to him the right to maintain a ferry. Judge Bull, of Black Rock, became a part owner of the ferry, and now owns the land on the American shore opposite the ferry landing. The rent was $200 per year, payable to the Common School Fund of Black Rock; in 1853 the State granted to the City of Buffalo exclusive power over all ferries within its limits, with the right to license and regulate the same.

An apology is due to you for this paper upon a subject so dry and uninteresting, but as the history of our city will necessarily require some mention of the old ferry, it is not beyond the province of the Historical Society to gather and preserve the fragments contained in this attempt to trace its origin and history. With this paper I present to the Historical Society a map of the locality of which it is an imperfect record, prepared by Mr. Henry Lovejoy from an actual survey, and from his own recollection of the old ferry at the Black Rock. It will form an interesting and valuable memorial of a part of our city which, but for his industrious and generous effort, would have found no memorial of its pristine importance.

www.ingramcontent.com/pod-product-compliance
Lightning Source LLC
LaVergne TN
LVHW010834120826
845149LV00016B/1369

* 9 7 8 1 4 1 8 1 8 9 7 4 7 *